GHOST RIDER THE RETURN OF BLAZE

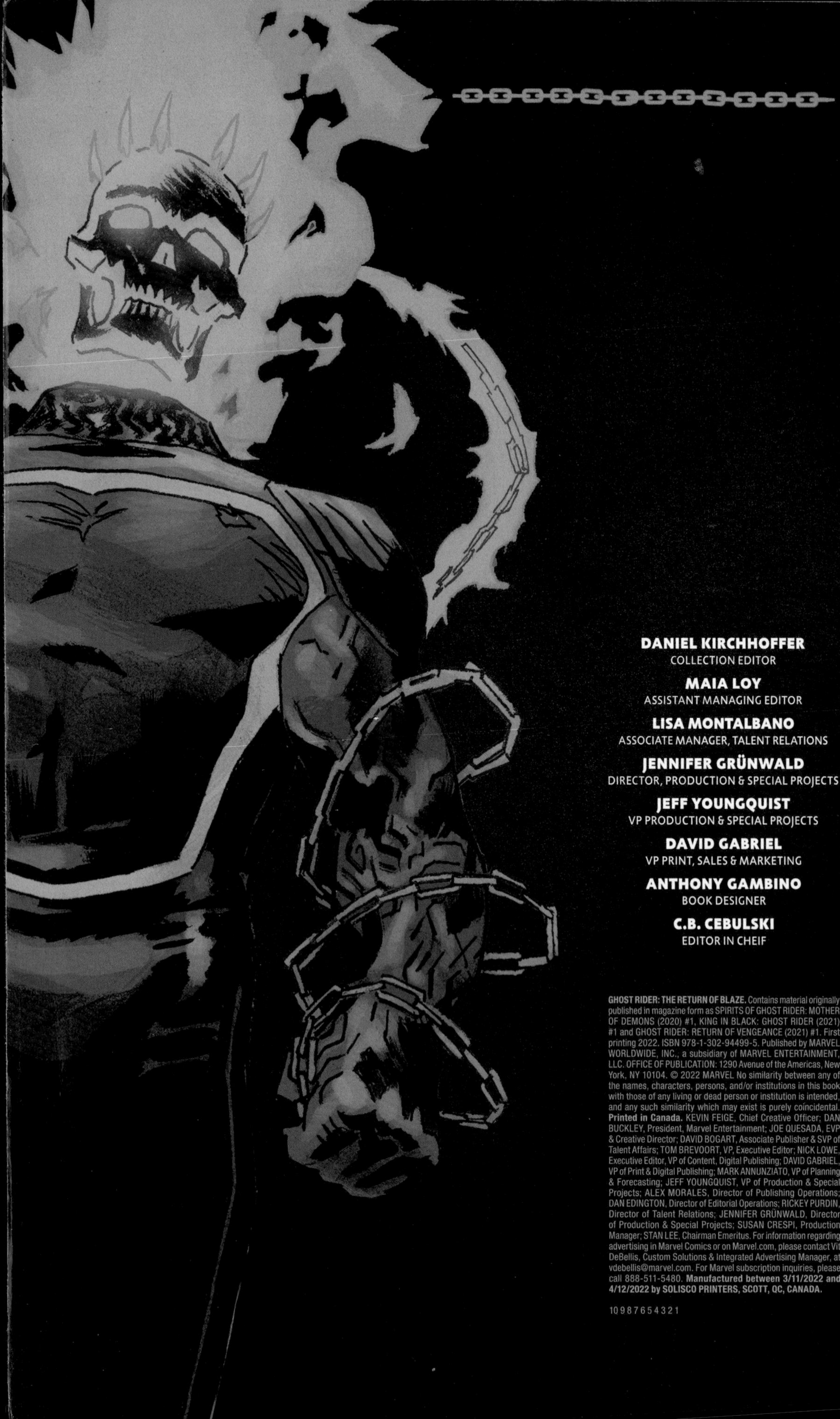

DANIEL KIRCHHOFFER
COLLECTION EDITOR

MAIA LOY
ASSISTANT MANAGING EDITOR

LISA MONTALBANO
ASSOCIATE MANAGER, TALENT RELATIONS

JENNIFER GRÜNWALD
DIRECTOR, PRODUCTION & SPECIAL PROJECTS

JEFF YOUNGQUIST
VP PRODUCTION & SPECIAL PROJECTS

DAVID GABRIEL
VP PRINT, SALES & MARKETING

ANTHONY GAMBINO
BOOK DESIGNER

C.B. CEBULSKI
EDITOR IN CHEIF

GHOST RIDER: THE RETURN OF BLAZE. Contains material originally published in magazine form as SPIRITS OF GHOST RIDER: MOTHER OF DEMONS (2020) #1, KING IN BLACK: GHOST RIDER (2021) #1 and GHOST RIDER: RETURN OF VENGEANCE (2021) #1. First printing 2022. ISBN 978-1-302-94499-5. Published by MARVEL WORLDWIDE, INC., a subsidiary of MARVEL ENTERTAINMENT, LLC. OFFICE OF PUBLICATION: 1290 Avenue of the Americas, New York, NY 10104. **Printed in Canada.** KEVIN FEIGE, Chief Creative Officer; DAN BUCKLEY, President, Marvel Entertainment; JOE QUESADA, EVP & Creative Director; DAVID BOGART, Associate Publisher & SVP of Talent Affairs; TOM BREVOORT, VP, Executive Editor; NICK LOWE, Executive Editor, VP of Content, Digital Publishing; DAVID GABRIEL, VP of Print & Digital Publishing; MARK ANNUNZIATO, VP of Planning & Forecasting; JEFF YOUNGQUIST, VP of Production & Special Projects; ALEX MORALES, Director of Publishing Operations; DAN EDINGTON, Director of Editorial Operations; RICKEY PURDIN, Director of Talent Relations; JENNIFER GRÜNWALD, Director of Production & Special Projects; SUSAN CRESPI, Production Manager; STAN LEE, Chairman Emeritus. For information regarding advertising in Marvel Comics or on Marvel.com, please contact Vit DeBellis, Custom Solutions & Integrated Advertising Manager, at vdebellis@marvel.com. For Marvel subscription inquiries, please call 888-511-5480. **Manufactured between 3/11/2022 and 4/12/2022 by SOLISCO PRINTERS, SCOTT, QC, CANADA.**

10 9 8 7 6 5 4 3 2 1

THE RETURN OF BLAZE

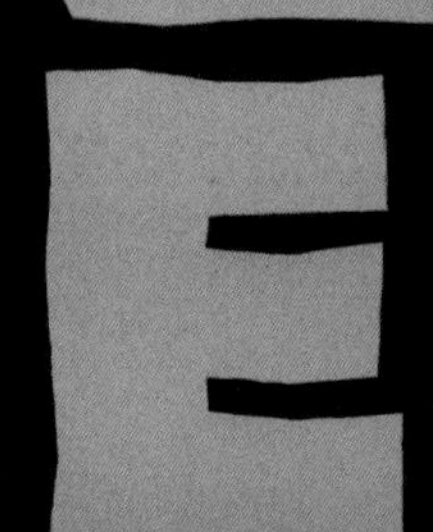

Spirits of Ghost Rider: Mother of Demons

ED BRISSON WRITER
ROLAND BOSCHI ARTIST
DAN BROWN COLORIST
VC's JOE CARAMAGNA LETTERER
PHILIP TAN &
JAY DAVID RAMOS COVER ART

Ghost Rider: King in Black

ED BRISSON WRITER
JUAN FRIGERI ARTIST
JASON KEITH COLORIST
VC's JOE CARAMAGNA LETTERER
WILL SLINEY &
CHRIS SOTOMAYOR COVER ART

Ghost Rider: Return of Vengeance

HOWARD MACKIE WRITER
JAVIER SALTARES ARTIST
JAVIER SALTARES (PG. 1-10) &
MARC DEERING (PG. 11-25) INKERS
ARIF PRIANTO COLORIST
VC's JOE SABINO LETTERER
JAVIER SALTARES &
EDGAR DELGADO COVER ART

SPECIAL THANKS: **MARK PANICCIA** & **CHRIS ROBINSON**

SHANNON ANDREWS BALLESTEROS
ASSISTANT EDITOR

CHRIS ROBINSON, **JAKE THOMAS** & **MARK BASSO**
EDITORS

SPIRITS OF GHOST RIDER:
MOTHER OF DEMONS #1

I WAS THERE AT THE START. ON MY FIRST BODY THEN.
WHEN GOD SOUGHT TO CREATE A PARADISE ON EARTH.
TO EXPAND HIS DOMAIN.

AS THOUGH WE WOULD LET SUCH ACTIONS GO UNCHECKED.
A WORLD WITHOUT HELL'S INFLUENCE HARDLY FEELS LIKE A PLACE WORTH LIVING.
AND SO I BORE ADAM THE FIRST MAN'S CHILDREN. CHILDREN THAT WOULD ONE DAY RUN THIS WORLD.

BUT GOD DIDN'T SHARE MY VISION AND DID NOT APPRECIATE THE COMPETITION.

AFTER A SHORT PERIOD, HE SENT HIS ANGELS TO KILL MY CHILDREN AND BANISHED ME FROM EDEN.

HE BANISHED ME BACK TO HELL.
AND PAIRED ADAM WITH A MORE SUITABLE...MORE MALLEABLE PARTNER.
BUT I HAVE A PARTNER AS WELL. AND HE HAS A PARTICULAR AFFINITY FOR THE MALLEABLE.
THE TWO OF US. A TEAM.
UNSTOPPABLE.

AS TIME PROGRESSED, IT SEEMED AS THOUGH MEPHISTO TOOK MORE INTEREST IN HUMANS.
TWISTING THEIR WORDS AGAINST THEM AND SETTING THEM FREE TO SORT THROUGH THEIR OWN ANGUISH AND GRIEF.
MORE AND MORE, HE NEGLECTED HIS DUTIES. FOUND EXCUSES TO ROAM EARTH, SEARCHING FOR MORE SOULS TO TORMENT.
AS THOUGH HELL WAS NOT ALREADY TEEMING WITH SOULS.
THEN JOHNNY BLAZE AND DR. STRANGE MANAGED TO CAPTURE MEPHISTO ON EARTH.
TO TRAP HIM THERE.
IT WAS ALMOST AS THOUGH THAT WAS WHAT HE WANTED. TO BE FREE OF THIS PLACE FOR ONCE.
TO LET SOMEONE ELSE TAKE THE REINS.
HOTEL INFERNO

AND THERE HE SITS. THE ILLOGICAL END TO MEPHISTO'S FASCINATION WITH HUMANKIND.
JOHNNY BLAZE. THE FALSE KING.
THE SERVANT.
MEPHISTO'S LITTLE FLESHY PLAYTHING.
SITTING ON A THRONE THAT SHOULD RIGHTFULLY BE MINE.
JOHNNY BLAZE...
...THESE DEMONS...THEY WON'T QUIT. THEY'LL KEEP COMING AT YOU AS LONG AS MEPHISTO IS OUT THERE. AS LONG AS HE BREATHES, THEY'LL NEVER RESPECT YOU AS THEIR KING.
THE LONGER HE'S AWAY FROM HELL, THE WEAKER HE IS. THE MORE VULNERABLE. IF YOU WERE TO GO TO HIM, YOU COULD END THIS. END HIM.

FWOOOOOSH
I DON'T HAVE ANY INTEREST IN MAKING DEALS WITH YOU, LILITH.
DON'T TRY TO SIDLE UP TO ME, WHISPERING IN MY EAR, AND THINK THAT I'LL FORGET WHAT YOU ARE.
MY APOLOGIES, KING.
HOW QUICKLY ONE FORGETS THEIR STATION.
BUT THERE IS MORE THAN ONE WAY TO WREST THE THRONE FROM THIS INTERLOPER.

LIMBO.
LILITH.
SURELY YOUR NEW MASTER WOULDN'T APPROVE OF YOU BEING HERE.
HE IS NOT MY MASTER.
AND IT WASN'T SO LONG AGO THAT YOUR OWN KINGDOM WAS USURPED BY A TEENAGED GIRL, SO PERHAPS WE CAN PUT THIS PETTINESS ASIDE AND TALK FOR A MOMENT.
WHY WOULD I LISTEN TO A WORD THAT COMES FROM YOUR FORKED TONGUE, WOMAN?
ALLOW ME TO APPROACH. THESE ARE NOT WORDS FOR ANY BUT YOU.
VERY WELL.

KNOW THAT IF YOU TRY ANYTHING, THE SPIRIT OF CORRUPTION SHALL STRIKE YOU DOWN.
I COME BEARING NO ILL WILL. ONLY A PROMISE OF SOMETHING BETTER.
AN OPPORTUNITY FOR US TO COMBINE OUR POWERS.
TO BECOME SOMETHING MORE POWERFUL.
SOMETHING THAT CAN'T BE WRESTED FROM US BY ANY HUMAN...
...NOR GOD.
A WORLD WHERE ALL HELLS ARE UNDER OUR CONTROL.
A KINGDOM RULED BY ONE KING AND ONE QUEEN.
THIS...THIS VIOLATES THE VERY SPIRIT OF THE PACT BETWEEN HELLS.
WE ARE DEVILS AND DEMONS...

"...VIOLATING SPIRITS IS WHAT WE DO."
HELL.
GUH, HOW MANY MORE LEVELS TO GO?
MAYBE IT'S TIME I STOP MESSING WITH KING BLAZE...
DON'T KNOW THAT I CAN TAKE HIM FIRIN' ME DOWN INTO THE DEPTHS AGAIN.
FEELS LIKE I'VE BEEN CLIMBING FOREVER.
I CAN HELP YOU FIND WHAT YOU'R LOOKING FOR.

I CAN HELP YOU GET OUT OF HERE. I CAN SEND YOU BACK TO EARTH, IF THAT'S WHAT YOU DESIRE.
YEAH? AND WHAT DO YOU GET OUT OF IT, LADY?
I GET ALL OF THIS.

"I GET HELL."
THE PLANS ARE IN MOTION, BUT MY BODY IS FAILING ME.
IT'S REACHED THE END OF ITS LIFE.
UNGGGH...
NGGGH...
AND SO...
...I BIRTH ANOTHER.

A NEW BODY FOR A NEW ERA.
ALL HAIL THE QUEEN.

THIS WAS SUPPOSED TO BE TEMPORARY.
SIT ON THE THRONE UNTIL STRANGE FIGURES OUT HOW TO DEAL WITH MEPHISTO.
THEN HE STAGES A BREAKOUT. GETS ME BACK WHERE I BELONG.
KING.
WHAT IS IT, D'KAY?
IT SEEMS THAT THERE IS... THERE IS AN UPRISING ON THE SIXTH LEVEL. YOUR ATTENTION IS REQUIRED.
I DON'T KNOW HOW LONG I'VE BEEN WAITING.

HOURS.
DAYS.
WEEKS.
YEARS.
CENTURIES?
SHOW ME.
I DON'T KNOW. TIME MOVES DIFFERENTLY DOWN HERE.

OWEVER LONG I'VE
EEN HERE FOR...IT'S
EEN LIKE THIS FOR
VERY SINGLE DAY.
NONSTOP REBELLIONS AND UPRISINGS. DEMONS ANGRY THAT I'M IN CHARGE.
I DO NOT BELONG HERE!
I DEVOTED MY LIFE TO A HIGHER POWER AND WILL NOT SUBMIT TO ANY MORE OF THE DEVIL'S TRICKERY. I WILL FIGHT HIM TO A BLOODY PULP.
THEIR MOTIVES MAY NOT BE THE SAME, BUT THEY ALL WANT THE SAME THING...
...THE SAME THING I WANT:
OUT.
THEY'RE GAINING MOMENTUM, SIR.
DEMONS ARE JOINING FORCES. THEY SEEK TO USURP YOU.
I CAN SEE THAT.

SINCE GETTING HERE...
...SINCE TAKING ON THE ROLE OF KING OF HELL...
...I'VE HAD A TARGET ON MY BACK.
YOU!
SHOULD HAVE KNOWN THAT YOU WOULD BE BEHIND THIS, DEMON.
HALF THE SOULS DOWN HERE ARE THOSE THAT I'VE PUT HERE.
I'VE SLAIN MANY A HERETIC AND EVIL SPIRIT IN SERVICE OF MY LORD.
AND THEY HAVEN'T FORGOTTEN.
AND I WILL SLAY THOUSANDS MORE, IF THAT'S WHAT IS REQUIRED TO PROVE MY DEVOTION TO HIM.
TO EARN MY PLACE NEXT TO HIM IN--
YOU'RE IN HELL, DEACON. WHERE YOU BELONG.
AND HERE, IN THIS PLACE, I AM YOUR LORD.
LIES!

WHICH IS WORSE, BLAZE...
...THE ONE BORN TO BE THE DEVIL...
...OR THE ONE WHO ILLINGLY KES UP THE MANTLE?
TAKE THEM AWAY.
SEND THEM TO THE BOTTOM-MOST LAYER. LET THE PARASITES OF PESTILENCE CHEW THEIR EYES AND NEST IN THEIR ORGANS.
I DO NOT WANT TO SEE THEIR FACES AGAIN.

EACH DEMON HAS A DIFFERENT REASON FOR FIGHTING ME.
SOME ARE LOYAL TO MEPHISTO.
SOME WANT TO ESCAPE.
SOME WANT MY THRONE.
AND SO I HAVE TO SHOW THEM.
SHOW THEM THAT I AM NOT TO BE MESSED WITH.
THAT THEY DO NOT CHALLENGE THE KING.
AND WITH EACH VICTORY...
...I CAN FEEL MY POWER GROWING.
C'MON, MAN! YOU KNOW HOW MUCH IT SUCKS DOWN HERE. JUST LET US GO!
I FEEL MORE...AT HOME.

THE SOULS TRAPPED DOWN HERE.
I DEFEAT THEM. I FEED ON THEIR SIN. I BECOME STRONGER.
BUT NO ONE DIES HERE.
THEY'RE ALREADY DEAD. THERE'S NO DYING AGAIN.
INSTEAD, THEY'RE SENT DOWN TO THE BOTTOM RUNGS OF HELL.
HOW DEEP THAT IS, I DON'T KNOW. I'VE NEVER BEEN BELOW THE EIGHTH LEVEL, BUT I HEAR WHISPERS OF HUNDREDS MORE.
MAYBE THOUSANDS MORE.
HOWEVER FAR DOWN IT IS... THAT'S WHERE THEY GO.
AND OVER DAYS, YEARS, CENTURIES...
HOW LONG HAVE I BEEN HERE?
...THEY FIGHT THEIR WAY BACK.

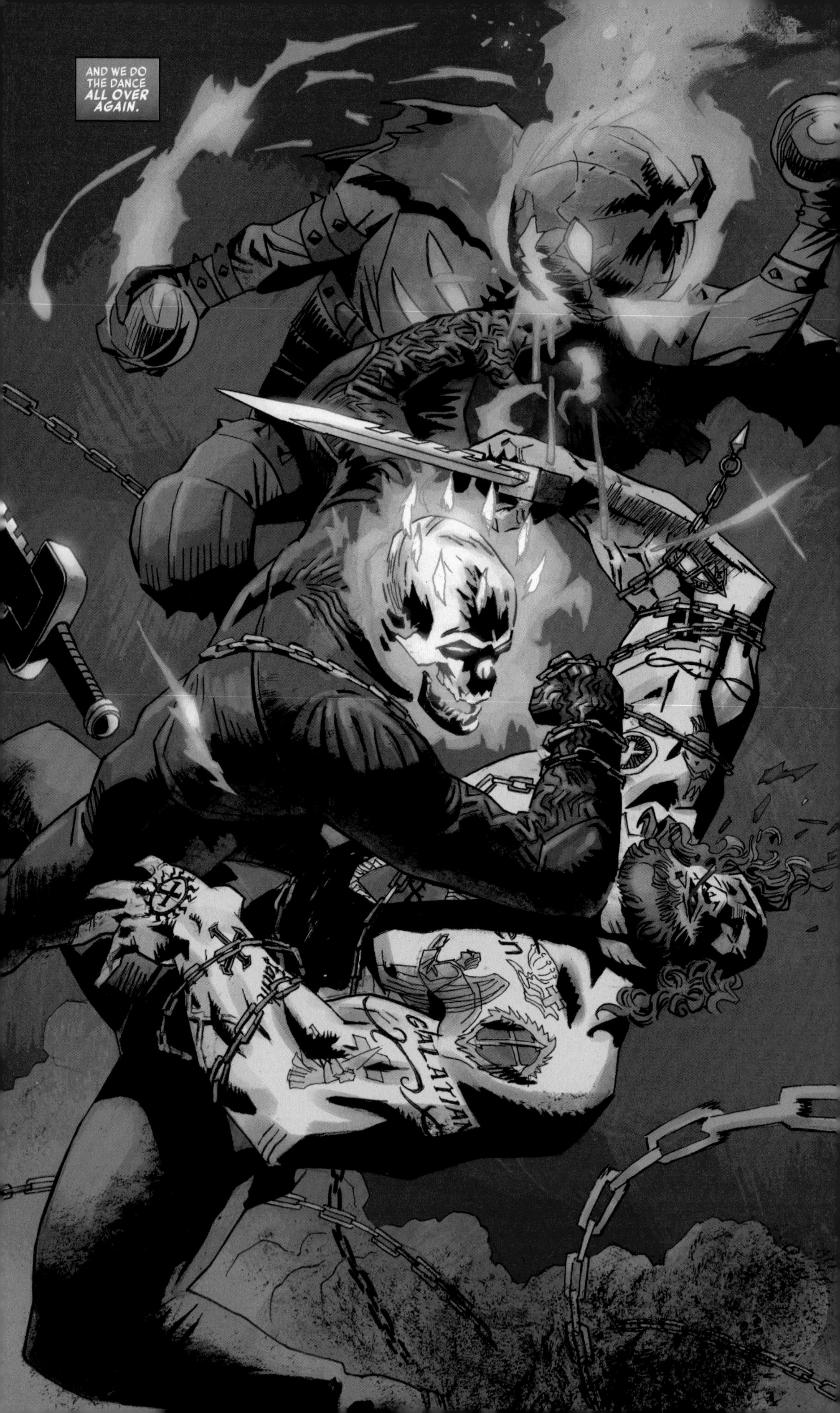
AND WE DO THE DANCE *ALL OVER AGAIN.*

YOU CAN KEEP COMING AT ME.
MAYBE IT'S BEEN EONS SINCE I ARRIVED.
DR. STRANGE, WONG, EVERYONE...
BUT I WILL KEEP BEATING YOU DOWN.
...THEY COULD BE DEAD FOR ALL I KNOW.
AND I WILL MAKE SURE THAT YOUR TIME HERE IS AS PAINFUL AS POSSIBLE.
SOME OF YOU...SOME OF YOU ARE HOLDING OUT HOPE THAT MEPHISTO MIGHT COME BACK ONE DAY.
BUT LET ME MAKE ONE THING CLEAR--
SO THIS IS IT. THIS IS ME NOW.
--MEPHISTO WILL NEVER SIT ON THIS THRONE AGAIN.
THIS THRONE IS MINE...

...AND I AM THE KING OF HELL.
ALL HAIL THE KING!
ROL

GAAAAAH!
DANNY!
ROOKLYN.
OW.
WHAT HAPPENED?
I FOUND BELASCO. I FOUND THE SPIRIT OF CORRUPTION.
BUT HE... HE WOULDN'T HELP. HE MADE ME FIGHT IT, THEN HE KILLED IT AND HE TURNED ME INTO THIS THING AND SENT ME BACK HERE.
WHAP
GET YOUR HANDS OFF ME!
YOU... YOU KNEW HE WOULD, DIDN'T YOU?

DANNY...THE THINGS WE'RE DEALING WITH...
I...WE **NEEDED** BELASCO'S HELP. WE **NEED** THE SPIRIT OF CORRUPTION IF WE'RE GOING TO **STOP** JOHNNY.

AND THAT MEANT A SACRIFICE.
YOU'VE BEEN A CONDUIT FOR A SPIRIT, YOU KNOW HOW TO CONTROL THESE THINGS.

THERE WAS A CHANCE YOU WOULDN'T MAKE IT BACK, BUT EVERY SOUL ON THE PLANET IS AT STAKE.
IT WAS A RISK I NEEDED TO TAKE.
NO.
I'M **DONE** WITH THIS! WITH ALL OF IT...
DANNY-- DON'T! WE **STILL** NEED TO--
I'M **THROUGH** BEING PLAYED, CARETAKER!

YOU'RE A DAMNED SUCKER, DANNY.
YOU HAD WHAT YOU WANTED.

JOHNNY HAD STRIPPED YOU OF THE SPIRIT OF VENGEANCE.
YOUR LIFE WAS YOURS AGAIN, AND YOU HAD TO...

...YOU JUST COULDN'T LEAVE IT ALONE.

LIQUORS · WINES
AND NOW YOU'RE TRAPPED... TRAPPED WITH WHATEVER THIS IS.

YOU DAMNED IDIOT.

EH YO...
...GIVE ME A BOTTLE OF BOURBON.
WE GOT LOTS OF BOURBON. WHAT KIND?
WHATEVER'S CHEAP AND BURNS GOING DOWN.

OLD BURNING BUCK BOURBON

WHAP WHAP WHAP WHAP WHAP
HEY MAN! YOU CAN'T DRINK THAT IN HERE! TAKE IT OUT TO THE ALLEY!

HEYA, DANNY...
GREAT.

SPICED
PUMPKIN
...CAN GHOST RIDER COME OUT AND PLAY?
JACK
Old No 7

HATE TO TELL YOU, JACK O'LANTERN, YOU'RE TOO LATE.
I AIN'T A GHOST RIDER NO MORE.

BESIDES, THOUGHT YOU WERE SUPPOSED TO BE DEAD ALREADY.
BEEN DEAD ABOUT AS MUCH AS I BEEN ALIVE.
BUT I FOUND ME A TICKET OUTTA HELL-- DID SOME TRADESIES. GOTTA DO A JOB TO PAY IT BACK.
DID YOU KNOW THERE WERE LIKE THREE OTHER GUYS RUNNING AROUND, WEARING MY CLOTHES, USING MY NAME?

THERE OUGHTA BE A LAW.

DING DING
HEY, WHERE YOU GOING?
LIKE I SAID...

LIQUORS
...I'M NOT GHOST RIDER.
GO FIND SOMEONE ELSE TO PUNC DOWN ON YOU.

HEY!
LIQ OR WINES
I DON'T CARE IF YOU ARE OR IF YOU AIN'T INTERESTED.
I WAS SENT HERE TO TAKE YOUR SORRY, SAD ASS OUT.
SO GET UP...

WHAK
...AND FIGHT ME.
UNGFF!

DAMMIT.
DAMMIT. DAMMIT. DAMMIT. DAMMIT.
I CAN FEEL IT INSIDE. WHATEVER THE HELL IT WAS THAT BELASCO PUT IN ME. THE SPIRIT OF CORRUPTION. THE SWORD...

SKLUCH
...IT HUNGERS.

IT WANTS TO FEED.
WHOA.
WHAT THE HELL?
THIS IS NEW.
YOU SHOULD HAVE JUST WALKED AWAY, JACK O'LANTERN.
OKAY.
YOU WARNED ME. I SHOULDA LISTENED.
YOU KNOW WHAT? I'LL JUST...
YEAH, I'M JUST GOING TO GO.

WHO
SENT
YOU?
KRUNK!
THAT WAS DUMB OF ME.
OKAY, OKAY. TELL YOU WHAT. I JUST GOT BACK TO, LIKE, BEING ALIVE. OKAY?
I TELL YOU WHO SENT ME, WE PART WAYS AND YOU TAKE THIS UP WITH HER.
OKAY?
WHO?!
FEEL THE SINKING DESPAIR OF MY--
SAVE THE POETRY. IT WAS LILITH.
SHE SAID THERE'S SOME SORT OF WAR COMING AND SHE WANTS YOU OUT OF THE WAY AND...IT'S COOL. I'LL GO BACK AND TELL HER THAT YOU AREN'T A GHOST RIDER ANYMORE AND I'M SURE--

UGGGK...
DON'T BOTHER.
LILITH...
...HAVEN'T HEARD THAT NAME IN AGES.
IF SHE'S BACK...
MAAAAAN...
I'LL TELL HER MYSELF.
...THEN JOHNNY'S IN MORE TROUBLE THAN I REALIZED.
DAMMIT, WHY CAN'T I EVER JUST WALK AWAY?

KING IN BLACK:
GHOST RIDER #1

KING IN BLACK
GHOST RIDER

RECENTLY, JOHNNY BLAZE (A.K.A. GHOST RIDER AND THE CURRENT RULER OF HELL) HAS NOT BEEN HIMSELF. UNDER HIS RULE, DEMONS HAVE ESCAPED HELL AND WREAKED HAVOC ON EARTH. JOHNNY'S BEEN ROUNDING UP ALL THE DEMONIC JAIL BREAKERS, BUT IT SEEMS EVERY DEMON HE SENDS BACK TO HELL LEAVES BEHIND A PIECE OF EVIL WITHIN HIM. THAT'S A FIGHT NO ONE COULD WITHSTAND UNSCATHED, BUT THANKS TO DANNY KETCH AND DOCTOR STRANGE, THE DEMONIC HOLD OVER JOHNNY HAS FINALLY BEEN BROKEN.

NOW JOHNNY'S READY TO CONTINUE HIS MISSION: SAVE HUMANITY FROM HELL ON EARTH! BUT WHAT IF HELL HAS ALREADY ARRIVED? ENTER KNULL, THE SYMBIOTE GOD WHO HAS BROUGHT HIS BLACK-GOO ARMY TO TAKE OVER THE WORLD...

HELL HAS BROKEN LOOSE.
LITERALLY.
MY OWN ARROGANCE LED ME TO BELIEVE THAT RUNNING HELL WOULD BE...
...WELL, NOT EASY, NO.
THIS... UNFF...IS VERY UNCOMFORTABLE...
BUT, NAIVELY, I THOUGHT I COULD MAKE A CHANGE.
I REALIZE HOW STUPID IT SOUNDS. WHAT WAS I GOING TO DO, INTRODUCE A REHABILITATION PROGRAM IN HELL?
INSTEAD, HELL ROSE UP AGAINST ME IN REBELLION.
AND NOW LILITH IS OUT IN THE WILD, PLOTTING TO SEIZE CONTROL OF HELL FROM ME...
...WHILE HUNDREDS OF ESCAPED DEMONS RUN AMOK ON EARTH.
KEEP TALKING-- I CAN ALWAYS MAKE IT MUCH LESS COMFORTABLE, MEPHIST--
--OOOOOOOOOO!
WOOOOOSH

WHAT THE HELL...
...IS THAT?

THAT LOOKS BAD.
SHUT UP.
A SWARM OF DRAGONS HEADED TO NEW YORK.
EIGHT MILLION PEOPLE...SOME OF THEM INNOCENT EVEN...
...MAYBE...
...RIGHT IN THE CROSS- AIRS OF THOSE BLACK, OILY CREATURES.
THOUGH M SURE THOSE OPLE WILL BE . MAYBE THEY'RE FRIENDLY DRAGONS?
BESIDES, IT'S NOT YOUR PROBLEM ANYMORE, RIGHT? YOUR CONCERNS ARE HEAVEN AND HELL. THE MORTAL PLANE IS BEST LEFT TO...MORTALS.
IT'S BENEATH YOUR STATION.
I SAID...
...SHUT UP!

VRRRMMMMMM
MEPHISTO TAUNTS, BUT HE KNOWS--JUST AS I DO--
--I CAN'T TURN MY BACK ON THIS.
THERE IS NO SENSE IN STOPPING LILITH IF IT MEANS SACRIFICING THOUSANDS--MILLIONS--OF LIVES TO DO SO.
SKREEEEEEE
THE DEMONS WILL HAVE TO WAIT.

OKAY, OKAY...
...NOW WHAT?!
KASMASH

SMASH
YOU MANIACS! YOU NEARLY HIT MY--
SHUUUK
DON'T WORRY, MY FLESHY FRIEND.
WE WILL DEAL WITH THOSE "MANIACS."
HE IS HERE! THE FALSE KING AND MEPHISTO!
THEY HAVE TAKEN TO THE SKIES.
BRING THEM DOWN!
KILL THE FALSE KING!

OHNATHON!
BUSY TRYING TO KILL A DRAGON RIGHT NOW, MEPHISTO.
WELL, YOU BETTER FIGURE IT OUT QUICK, DRAGON SLAYER.
BECAUSE YOU HAVE A LOT OF EAGER CUSTOMERS HEADED YOUR WAY.
UGH. THE FEEL OF IT.
DON'T KNOW HOW VENOM IS INVOLVED IN ALL THIS, BUT YOU NEVER FORGET THE SLICK, SLITHERING FEEL OF A SYMBIOTE.
I PRAY THAT MY HELLFIRE CAN PROVIDE ENOUGH DISTRACTION...
...WHILE I...
FWOOOOOM
...GAMBLE EVERYTHING ON A HAIL MARY.

NOT SURE THIS THING HAS MUCH OF A SOUL.
NO IDEA IF THE DAMNATION STARE IS GOING TO DO SQUAT.
BUT MAYBE I GET LUCKY AND IT SENDS THIS BASTARD RIGHT TO HELL LIKE IT DOES TO THOSE DAMNED RUNAWAY DEMONS.
STARE INTO MY EYES.
FEEL THE SOUL-SCORCH WRATH OF M DAMNATION STARE.
FEEL THE PAIN OF EVERY WRONG YOU HAVE EVER--
OOOF.
SKRAAAAAAAWWW!
FORGOT HOW MUCH USING THE STARE ON A SYMBIOTE TAKES OUT OF ME. HURTS ME ALMOST AS MUCH AS IT HURTS THEM.
NEED A SECOND TO RECOUP.
DAMNATION STARE BROKE OFF WHATEVER SORT OF CONNECTION THIS DRAGON HAD TO THE OTHERS. THAT'S SOMETHING, AT LEAST.
BOUGHT MYSELF A FEW MINUTES, MAYBE.
A FEW MINUTES TO FIGURE OUT HOW THE HELL...
...TO KILL A SYMBIOTE-INFECTED DRAGON.
SHUUUUUK
WHAT...?

SKRRRAAAAAAAAAW!
HEY, BROTHER.
LOOKS LIKE YOU COULD USE A HAND.

DANNY?
CALL ME DEATH RIDER.
DEATH RIDER? ARE YOU SERIOUS?
I DIDN'T WANT TO USE THE LAST GUY'S NAME. I MEAN, "NECROSIS"?* COME ON.
BESIDES, DEATH RIDER FEELS MORE ON BRAND, RIGHT? GHOST RIDER, DEATH RIDER...
OKAY, OKAY. DEATH RIDER IT IS.
YOU'RE DAMN RIGHT.
*SEE GHOST RIDER (2019) #4! --ED
THOUGHT THAT WAS A DRAGON INFECTED BY A SYMBIOTE.
BUT LOOK AT THIS.
IT WAS A SYMBIOTE IN THE FORM OF A DRAGON.
IT TRIED TO INFECT ME BUT COULDN'T. I DON'T KNOW IF THAT'S BECAUSE OF MY CONNECTION TO HELL OR BECAUSE OF THE DAMNATION STARE.
EITHER WAY, DON'T GET NEAR IT.
YOUR BLIGHT BLADE ONLY STUNNED THE SYMBIOTE. ALREADY, IT'S PULLING BACK TOGETHER.
THEN WE NEED TO FIND A WAY TO KILL IT...
...BECAUSE THAT WAS ONLY ONE OF ABOUT A THOUSAND SWARMING THE CITY.
WAIT...
...WHAT IS BLACKHEART DOING HERE?!

PLEASE. DO YOU THINK YOUR CHAINS CAN HOLD ME?
ARE YOU COMING TO TRY TO SNATCH MY CROWN TOO?
I'M HERE TO END THIS RIDICULOUS WAR.
TO STOP YOU BEFORE ANY MORE DIE.

JOHNNY.
LET HIM GO.
AND YOU!
YOU SHOULD KNOW BETTER THAN TO BE CHUMMING IT UP WITH BLACKHEART.
SAYS THE MANIAC RIDING AROUND WITH MEPHISTO.
JUST...
...SHUT UP FOR A MINUTE AND LET US EXPLAIN.

THAT WENT WELL.
GHOST RIDERS HAVE NEVER BEEN KNOWN FOR THEIR EVEN TEMPERAMENT, CARETAKER.
I'M WELL AWARE.
YOU KNOW, FOR SOMEONE WHO TOLD ME THAT THEY DIDN'T WANT TO BE INVOLVED IN THIS WAR--
I KNOW, I KNOW. BUT PLEASE JUST LISTEN.
BLACKHEART'S HERE BECAUSE HE WANTS TO KEEP LILITH FROM TAKING THE THRONE OF HELL.
SURE HE DOES.
WANTS TO KEEP HER FROM IT SO THAT HE CAN CLAIM IT FOR HIMSELF.
THAT MAY BE, BUT THAT'S A BRIDGE WE'LL CROSS WHEN THE TIME COMES.
FOR NOW... HE...
HE HAS STACY AND EMMA. HE'S INFECTED THEIR SOULS, AND HE WON'T RELEASE THEM UNLESS WE HELP HIM END THIS WAR.
THEY'RE NOT PART OF THIS. THEY DON'T DESERVE TO DIE BECAUSE OF WHAT OUR LIVES HAVE BECOME.
STACY? YOUR EX-GIRLFRIEND?
IT'S A LONG STORY.
AND I DON'T EVEN KNOW WHO EMMA IS.
SHE WORKS AT MY BAR. SU THINKS SHE R THE PLACE. Y MET HER.
RIGHT. THE CHARMER.
AND HOW DOES BLACKHEART PROPOSE WE END THIS WAR?
YOU'RE NOT GOING TO LIKE IT.
COLOR ME SURPRISED.

IT INVOLVES MEPHISTO--
MEPHISTO?! DAMMIT!
I TURN AROUND FOR ONE SECOND AND...
HUFF HUFF
THAT'S RIGHT, KEEP BABBLING ON, YOU MORONS.
JUST NEED A FEW MORE MOMENTS TO GET THE HELL OUT OF HERE, THEN I'M ON THE FIRST PLANE TO FLORIDA FOR SUN AND FUN AND--

MOVE IT, FOOL!
MY KING!

PLEASE... WE ARE HERE TO HELP YOU.
WE ARE HERE TO...

...TO...
...GUUUUK...

...EAAAAT YOURRR SPIIIIIINE!

BACK.
THE DEVIL IS OURS.

WE NEED TO GET MEPHISTO AWAY FROM THE SYMBIOTE.

IF WE CAN'T *KILL* THE SYMBIOTE, WE NEED TO KEEP STUNNING IT. BUY OURSELVES SOME TIME TO FIGURE OUT A MORE *PERMANENT SOLUTION.*
WE WON'T SUCCEED BY STANDING HERE AND *OGLING* THE THREAT.
YOU KEEP THEM OCCUPIED. I WILL TEND TO MY FATHER.

JOHNNY... THIS SYMBIOTE... ALL THESE DEMONS...
...THEY'RE ALL INFECTED BY ONE ORGANISM. IF YOU USE YOUR DAMNATION STARE ON ONE, THEN THE REST SHOULD FALL TOO.
SURE, BUT IT WON'T BUY US MUCH TIME, AND I DON'T KNOW THAT I CAN DO IT MORE THAN ONCE MORE.
LAST TIME, FELT LIKE MY HEAD WAS GOING TO EXPLODE.
WE JUST NEED A LITTLE ROOM TO BREATHE.
BLAM
HURRY.
LOOK INTO MY EYES.
FEEL THE--
NO!

WE WON'T LET YOU HURT US AGAIN.
UNFFF.
IT'S OUR TURN...
GOING TO SLURP THE SWEET MARROW FROM YOUR--
GUUUUUK.
THAT'S TWICE I'VE PULLED YOUR FAT FROM THE FIRE.
IN CASE YOU WERE COUNTING.
IT'S REAL GREAT THAT YOU TOOK DOWN ONE DEMON.
GET TO WORK ON THE OTHER THOUSAND!
BLAM

WATCH MY BACK--GIVE ME THE SPACE I NEED TO WORK.
THAT'S WHAT BROTHERS ARE FOR.
NGFFF. JOHNNY!
NO.
LOOK INTO MY EYES.
DON'T!
FEEL THE PAIN THAT YOU HAVI INFLICTED UPON OTHERS.
I BEG OF YOU!
FEEL THE SEARING SUFFERING AN UNYIELDING WRAT OF THE...
...DAMNATION STARE!
IT WORKE

ENOUGH OF THIS.

WHAT IS YOUR PURPOSE HERE? DO YOU WORK FOR LILITH?
AAAGGGH!

ANSWER ME!
PLEASE... PLEASE, MY LORD.
I AM BUT A HUMBLE SERVANT OF MEPHISTO.
I DO NOT STAND WITH LILITH.

SMART LITTLE DEMON.
TELL ME THAT YOU DID NOT COME HERE WITHOUT A PLAN.
YES...
...WE HAVE A PLAN.

THIS WAR ENDS HERE.

SHIIIK

YOUR SACRIFICE WILL NOT BE FORGOTTEN, LITTLE ONE.

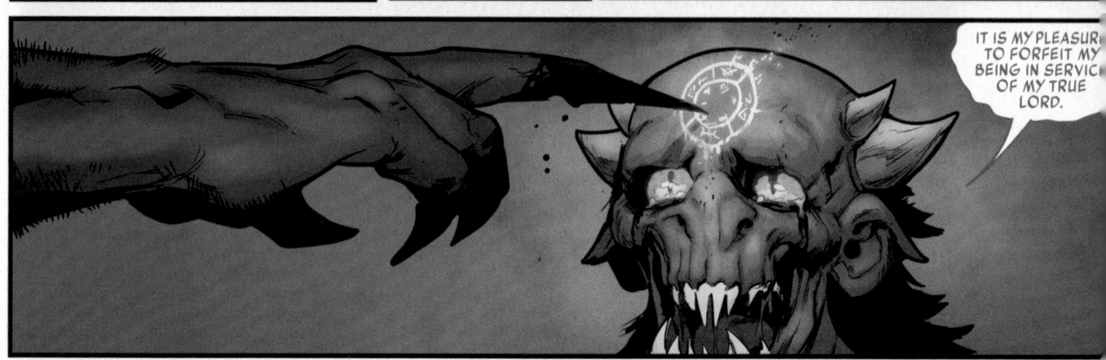
IT IS MY PLEASUR
TO FORFEIT MY
BEING IN SERVIC
OF MY TRUE
LORD.

AAAAAAARGGGGGH!
GRAAAAAAAAAAAAAAAAH!
AH, THE PORTAL OF 1,000 CONDEMNED SOULS...
VERY
CLEVE

MY SON. I KNEW YOU WOULD NOT FORSAKE ME.
IF I HAD A HEART, IT WOULD BE BURSTING WITH JOY.
I'VE ENJOYED MY LITTLE VACATION, BUT YOU KNOW WHAT THEY SAY.
THERE IS NO PLACE LIKE--
--HOOOOOOOOOOOOME.
SWIFFFF

DISTRACTING ME, MAKING A RUN.
IT'S GETTING OLD.
OOOF.
SO IS BEING CHAINED AND DRAGGED AROUND BY THE USURPER OF MY THRONE.
DO YOU HEAR ME COMPLAINING?

ALL.
THE.
TIME.
JOHNNY...

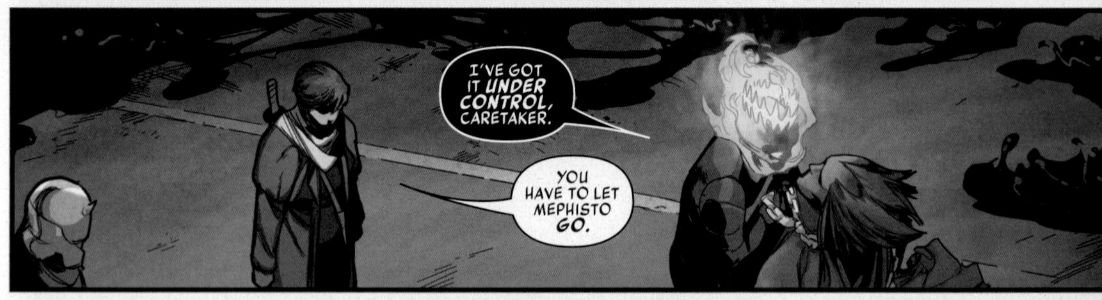

I'VE GOT IT UNDER CONTROL, CARETAKER.
YOU HAVE TO LET MEPHISTO GO.

MEPHISTO IS THE ONLY ONE WHO CAN LEAD ME TO LILITH'S ARMY OF DEMONS.
WITHOUT HIM, I'M NOT SURE I CAN DO THIS.
EVEN WITH HIM, YOU CAN'T.

THAT WHAT YOU THINK TOO, DEATH RIDER?
I DON'T LIKE IT EITHER.
BUT THE CARETAKER IS RIGHT.

MEPHISTO'S BEEN EALING WITH LILITH'S TTEMPTS TO TAKE OVER HELL FOR MILLENNIA.
YOU'VE BEEN IN HELL FOR MONTHS AND...
LOOK, THIS ISN'T WHAT YOU WANT TO HEAR, I KNOW...

BUT IF YOU LET MEPHISTO GO, LET HIM RECLAIM THE THRONE...
...YOU CAN END THIS NOW.
OH, I LIKE HER. SHE'S A SMART ONE. YOU SHOULD DEFINITELY LISTEN TO HER.
SHUT UP.

MEPHISTO...WE KNOW HOW HE OPERATES. WE'VE BATTLED HIM BEFORE. WE'LL BATTLE HIM AGAIN.
LILITH, HOWEVER...

IF SHE WINS... IF SHE KILLS YOU AND MANAGES TO SEIZE CONTROL OF HELL...
...SHE WON'T STOP THERE. SHE'S GOING TO RAISE HELL UP TO EARTH.
THE ENTIRE PLANET WILL BE DAMNED.

AFTER ALL I DID...
...FIGHTING TO TAKE HELL, TO CONTROL IT, TO REIN IT IN...
...YOU WANT ME TO JUST GIVE UP?
MEPHISTO IS BEHIND EVERY NASTY THING THAT I'VE EVER HAD TO ENDURE.
IT'S BECAUSE OF HIM THAT I'VE BEEN CURSED TO THIS LIFE.
IT'S BECAUSE OF HIM THAT MY FAMILY IS DEAD.
AND HOW MANY OTHERS HAS HE DAMNED? HOW MANY LIVES HAS HE RUINED?
WHEN YOU FIRST CAME TO ME AND ASKED ME FOR HELP, I SHOULD HAVE LISTENED.
I SHOULD HAVE BEEN THERE FOR YOU SO THAT YOU DIDN'T HAVE TO GO THIS ALONE.
FOR THAT, I AM SORRY, JOHNNY.
TRULY, TRULY SORRY.
BUT GHOST RIDER IS NEEDED HERE.
YOU CAN CONTINUE TRYING TO SAVE THE SOULS OF EVERYONE IN THE WORLD--
--BUT IF WE DON'T STOP THIS THREAT, THERE WON'T BE A SOUL LEFT TO SAVE.
SEND MEPHISTO BACK TO HELL WHERE HE BELONGS. LET HIM SET HIS OWN HOUSE IN ORDER.
YOU'RE ASKING ME TO TAKE A PRETTY BIG LEAP OF FAITH IN THE SELF-PROCLAIMED PRINCE OF LIES.
I KNOW.
YOU HAVE MY WORD.
IF HE RENEGES ON HIS PROMISE...

"...I'LL GO DOWN TO HELL AND KILL HIM MYSELF."
PARTING IS SUCH SWEET SORROW.
I WILL MISS OUR TIME TOGETHER, JOHNNY.
AS ONE FINAL GIFT, ALLOW ME TO LEND A HAND...

...AND LESSEN YOUR BURDEN.

I'LL DISPOSE OF THIS SYMBIOTE IN THE CAULDRON OF THE INFINITE COSMIC FLAME.
A GIFT FROM DORMAMMU THAT HAS BEEN COLLECTING DUST SINCE THE BEGINNING OF TIME. IT WILL BE GOOD TO FINALLY PUT IT TO SOME USE.

TA-TA!

I HATE EVERYTHING ABOUT THIS.
CHOOSING THE DEVIL YOU KNOW OVER THE DEVIL YOU DON'T...
...IS STILL CHOOSING A DEVIL.
POOF
I KNOW.
I KNOW THAT THIS ISN'T THE ENDING YOU WANTED.
IT'S MESSY, AND WE ALL HOPED IT COULD GO A DIFFERENT WAY.
BUT SOMETIMES YOU HAVE TO TAKE WHAT YOU CAN GET.
THE IMPORTANT THING IS...

"...WE NEVER
STOP FIGHTING."

EPILOGUE: PART 1.
THE FADEAWAY.
BROOKLYN, NY.
FADEAWAY
FADEAWAY

WHA...WHAT... HAPPENED?
WE MUST'VE GONE HARD LAST NIGHT, STACY. I DON'T REMEMBER A THING.
I JUST WANT TO LIE HERE AND STARE AT THE CEILING AND NOT MOVE AND NOT BREATHE AND...
NOPE... PRETTY SURE I'M GONNA THROW UP.
I NEED TO GO HOME.
WAIT...WAS THERE, LIKE...SOME SORT OF DEMON-DUDE? LIKE EIGHT FEET TALL, RED GLOWING EYES AND SMELLED LIKE ROTTEN EGGS? OR WAS I JUST THAT DRUNK?
NO, YOU WEREN'T. I REMEMBER THAT TOO.
DAMN. THAT'S WEIRD, RIGHT? LIKE...
WORD OF ADVICE, EMMA.
YOU HANG AROUND DANNY TOO MUCH, THIS IS THE KIND OF THING YOU INVITE INTO YOUR LIFE.
THERE ARE A MILLION OTHER BARS IN NEW YORK. PLENTY OF JOBS FOR SOMEONE LIKE YOU.
YOU MIGHT WANT TO CONSIDER IT.
NOW, IF YOU'LL EXCUSE ME...
...I NEED TO CHECK ON MY FAMILY.

EPILOGUE. PART 2. HELL.
WELCOME HOME, MY LORD.
ALL HAIL MEPHISTO, THE ONE TRUE KING.
THIS IS QUITE THE WELCOME, BLACKHEART.

YOUR ABSENCE WAS LIKE A VOID, FATHER.
YOUR RETURN IS CAUSE FOR CELEBRATION.
YES, I DO LOVE A GOOD PARTY.
NEED TO SHAKE THE STINK OF EARTH AND HUMANS OFF OF ME.

AND THE SYMBIOTE?
SHOULD I BRING IT TO THE CAULDRON OF THE INFINITE COSMIC FLAME?
HA!

DON'T BE SO NAIVE.
THERE IS NO SUCH CAULDRON.
NO?
IT'S JUST A MASHING OF WORDS.
I WANTED OUT OF THERE AND THOUGHT THAT HAVING A SYMBIOTE OF OUR OWN MIGHT MAKE FOR SOME RAINY-DAY FUN IN THE FUTURE.
NOW BE A DEAR AND STORE THAT SYMBIOTE SOMEWHERE SECURE UNTIL THAT RAINY DAY.

AH...
...IT'S GOOD TO BE HOME.
END.

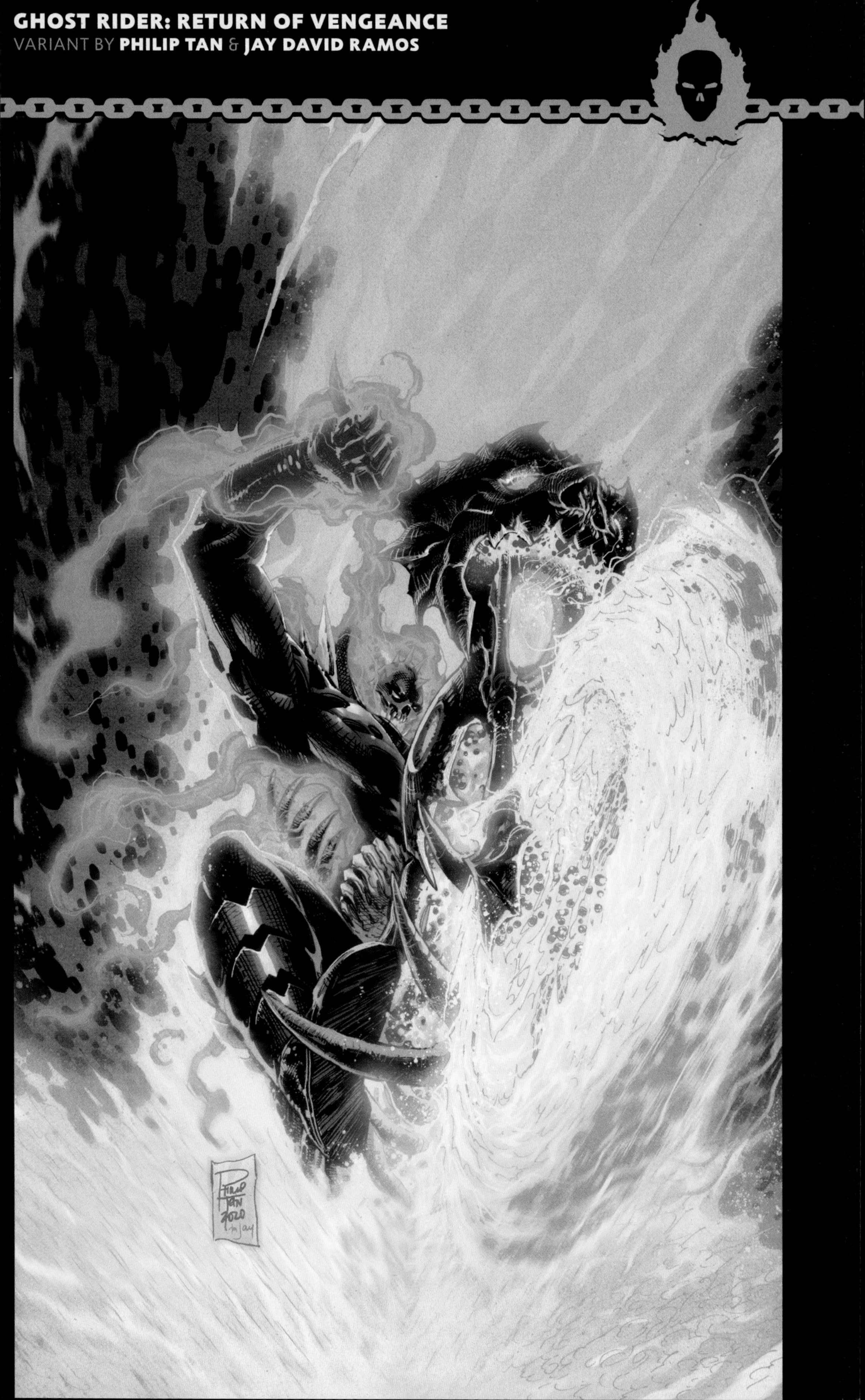
GHOST RIDER: RETURN OF VENGEANCE
VARIANT BY PHILIP TAN & JAY DAVID RAMOS

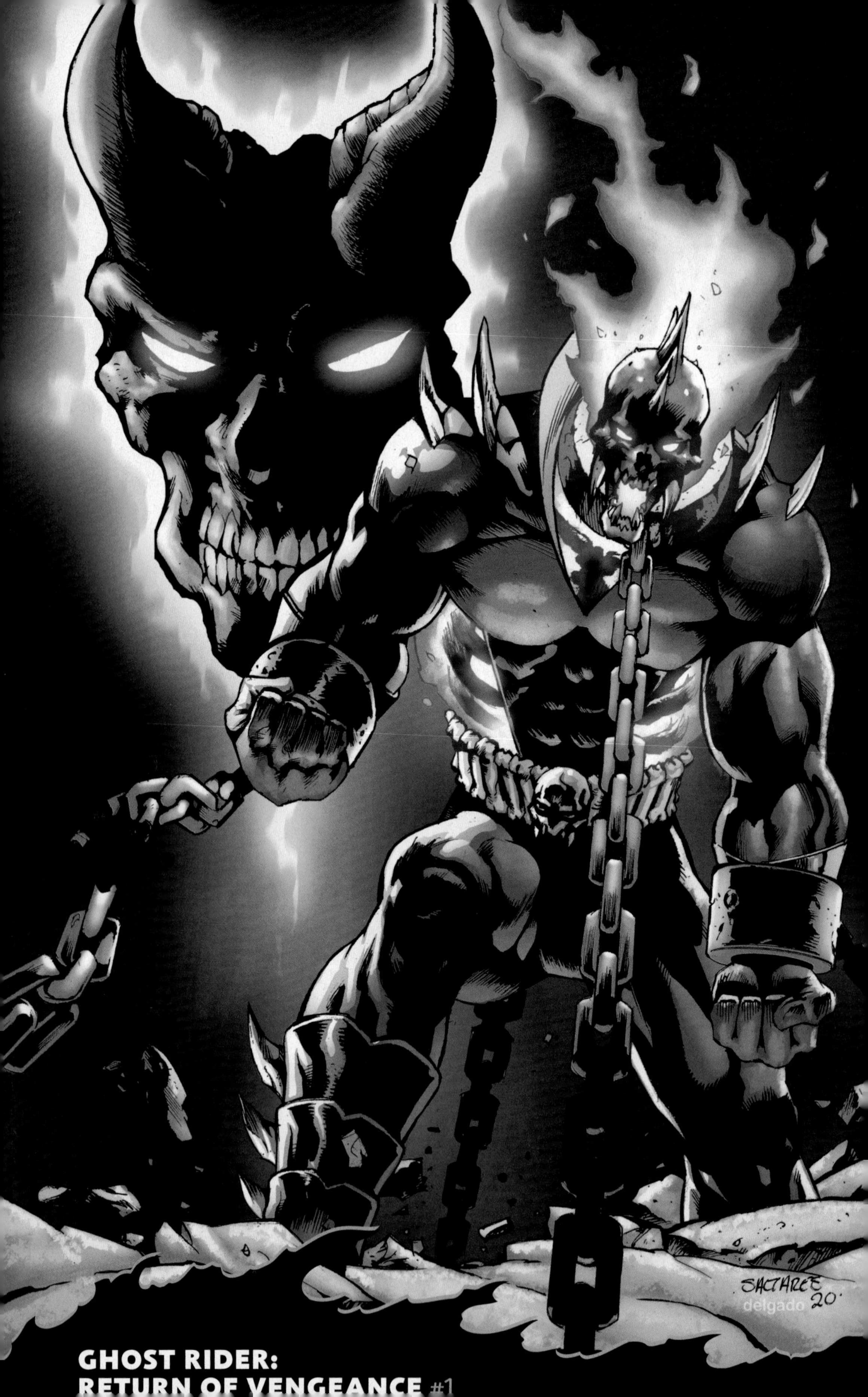
GHOST RIDER:
RETURN OF VENGEANCE #1
delgado

MICHAEL BADILINO...
...WELCOME TO MY PERSONAL CORNER OF HELL!
BADILINO?
THE LAST OF MY LIFE... MY HUMANITY... ARE LONG GONE.
ALL THAT'S LEFT IS...
...VENGEAN
IT'S WHO I AM.
IT'S WHAT DO.

I'VE KIND OF LOST TRACK OF TIME...HOW LONG HAVE I BEEN HERE?
TIME DOESN'T REALLY HAVE MUCH MEANING HERE, BUT NO WORRIES... I'LL HELP YOU REMEMBER EVERYTHING.
YOU'VE FINALLY BEEN KICKED DOWN TO ME AND MY UNIT.
ONLY THE DARKEST HEARTS AND BLEAKEST SOULS ARE DEEMED WORTHY OF MY SPECIAL ATTENTION. I'M R'ACK, AND YOU AND I ARE GOING TO GET TO KNOW EACH OTHER REAL WELL.
I THINK YOU MAY BE ACQUAINTED WITH ONE OR TWO OF YOUR FELLOW INMATES.
I KNOW YOU KNOW ANTON HELLGATE.
OBSESSED WITH HIS IMMORTALITY, HE VENTURED TOO FAR INTO THE DARKNESS AND EVENTUALLY WAS CONSUMED BY IT...AND NOW HE CAN LIVE IN HELL FOR ETERNITY.
SKINNER, SPAWN OF THE WITCH-DEMON MOTHER LILITH. A BETRAYER OF HIS OWN KIND...A DEMON-KILLER.
I HAVE PLANS FOR THE TWO OF YOU SHORTLY, BUT FIRST FOR THE FORMALITIES...
HELLGATE.
LET'S REVIEW YOUR SINS AND BEGIN YOUR TORTURE WITH... MEMORY.
"MICHAEL BADILINO. FORMERLY OF A POLICE TASK FORCE CHARGED WITH HUNTING DOWN A GHOST RIDER.
"YOU GOT A LITTLE TOO CLOSE TO HELLFIRE... AND YOU NOW KNOW YOU CAN GET BURNED.
"YOU DREW THE ATTENTION OF THE ONCE GREAT--AND NOW FALLEN--LORD OF HELL, MEPHISTO...

HOW'D THAT WORK OUT FOR YOU?
MEPHISTO ALWAYS IKED TO PLAY WITH IS VICTIMS, SO HE RICKED JOHNNY BLAZE INTO BLASTING YOUR FATHER WITH HELLFIRE.
"THE HELLFIRE DIDN'T CONSUME HIM...
"...BUT THE MADNESS DID.
"YOUR GRIEF WAS OVERWHELMING.
"AND THAT WAS WHAT DROVE YOU TO MAKE A DEAL WITH MEPHISTO HIMSELF. EXACTLY AS HE PLANNED.
"YOU WERE THE LATEST RIDER...AND YOU GUARANTEED YOURSELF A PLACE DOWN HERE ON THAT DAY.
"WHAT WOULD A PAWN OF HELL EXPECT?
"AS VENGEANCE, YOU BATTLED THE OTHER RIDERS... GHOST RIDER AND BLAZE AND CARETAKER HIMSELF.
"ULTIMATELY, YOU JOINED THESE MIDNIGHT SONS AND BETRAYED THE DARK FORCES FROM WHICH YOU DREW YOUR POWERS. YOU PROBABLY THOUGHT YOU COULD REDEEM YOURSELF? HA!
"AFTER HELLGATE TORTURED, TESTED, AND DROVE YOU TO THE EDGE OF INSANITY...

"...YOU WERE A HERO NO MORE.
"I HONESTLY THINK IT AMUSED MEPHISTO TO SEE YOU--VENGEANCE IN ITS PUREST FORM--UNLEASHED UPON THE WORLD OF MAN.
"BETRAYING EVERY ABSURD CODE THE FLAME-HEADED MORONS HAD CREATED FOR THEMSELVES."
AFTER ALL YOU DID...AFTER YOU TRIED TO BE A HERO...YOU STILL WOUND UP HERE...WITH US.
NO MATTER WHO'S IN CHARGE OF HELL--NONE OF US HAVE ANY USE FOR RIDERS.
SO, WE'VE SET UP A LITTLE WELCOME FOR YOU. A TASTE OF THINGS TO COME.
UNCHAIN HIM.
YOU UNCHAIN HIM!
HE MIGHT NOT BE WHO HE WAS, BUT WE'VE ALL GOT THE SCARS TO PROVE HE'S STILL GOT SOME HELL JUICE IN HIS BLOOD.
TCHINK
COWARDS. AFRAID OF A HUMAN?
HE'S NOT VENGEANCE ANYMORE. WITH THE MANACLES KEEPING HIM FROM TRANSFORMING, HE IS NOTHING BUT SOMETHING TO PLAY WITH.
NEW GUY!
FREE HIM UP FOR THE "INITIATION"!
M-M-ME?
CHAINS OFF... MANACLES ON. YOU'LL BE FINE.

HOLD
TILL...OR I'LL HURT YA.
I'M **STILL** OING TO HURT OU, BUT HOLD STILL!

GOOD. SHOW THEM WHO'S IN CHARGE AND THEY REALIZE THEY'RE NOTHING DOWN HERE.
RIGHT, BADILINO? YOU'RE **NOTHING!**
TODAY YOU'RE GOING TO FIGHT ANOTHER OF THE INMATES...AND IT BETTER BE ENTERTAINING.
I MIGHT BE NOTHING, BUT...

WHAT DOES THIS...
HUH?

...MAKE HIM?
KRAK
ARRRRR...

SPLUNCH
JUST A PILE OF DEMON GOO.
NOW STOP BORING ME AND LET'S GET THIS "INITIATION" OVER WITH.
BRING ME **HELLGATE!**

YOU DON'T GET TO CHOOSE ***ANYTHING*** DOWN HERE!
KRAK
I CHOOSE ***EVERYTHING*** THAT HAPPENS HERE. AND I CHOOSE...

...**SKINNER**.

I HEAR HE DID SOME NASTY STUFF WHEN MOMMY CALLED HIM BACK YEARS AGO.
NORMALLY I'D ADMIRE THAT KIND OF THING, BUT WE DON'T HAVE MUCH USE FOR LILITH'S BOOTLICKERS DOWN HERE THESE DAYS.
SKINNER, MAKE HIM BLEED.
TEACH MISTER FORMERLY-KNOWN-AS A GOOD ENOUGH LESSON AND I'LL TAKE A DAY OFF OF YOUR TORTURE.
A DAY?
THAT'S AN ETERNITY DOWN HERE!
FOR A WHOLE DAY...
...I'LL STRIP THE FLESH FROM HIS BODY AND KNIT YOU A SCARF WITH IT!

JUST MAKE IT ENTERTAINING...
...AND MAKE HIM SCREAM.
BADILINO, I'VE GOT A DEAL FOR YOU.
WHY SHOULD I MAKE A DEAL WITH YOU?
BECAUSE I CAN HELP YOU GET US BOTH OUT OF HERE... AND SETTLE YOUR SCORE WITH HELLGATE AT THE SAME TIME.
WHAT? HOW?
WITH THIS!
A SHARD OF GHOST RIDER'S HELLFIRE-INFUSED BONE.
BEEN KEEPING IT AS A MEMENTO...CARRYING THE SEARING PAIN UNDER MY FLESH FOR YEARS.
YOU KNOW YOU WANT IT... IT'LL BYPASS THE MANACLES KEEPING YOU FROM TRANSFORMING...
JUST TAKE IT...TOUCH IT... TRANSFORM...
...BECOME VENGEANCE AGAIN, AND WE CAN RIDE RIGHT OUT OF HERE.
I--
FWOOSH

VENGEANCE... THE RIDER...IT'S UNLEASHED!
WHAT DO WE DO? WHAT DO WE DO? WHAT DO WE DO?!
YOU SUFFER...AFTER I HEAR THE REST OF SKINNER'S PLAN.
STEP ONE IS GET RID OF MY SHACKLES.
SURE, BUT THE HELLFIRE MIGHT STING A LITTLE.
FWOOSH
ARRGH!
THANKS!
SWIK
STEP TWO... KILL AS MANY DEMONS AS YOU CAN.

WOOSH
FWOOSH
AIIIIE!
FWOOSH

LIKE THAT?
YEAH... EXACTLY LIKE THAT.
OH GOOD... I'D HATE TO DISAPPOINT A DEMON FROM HELL.
NO WORRIES, BUT I THINK YOU'RE GOING TO REALLY LIKE STEP THREE.

WAIT.
SOMETHING'S MISSING.

I CAN'T BE A RIDER...

FWOOSH

...WITHOUT MY *BIKE*.
SERIOUSLY... *THAT* IS IMPRESSIVE.
YOU DON'T WANT TO MAKE ANOTHER FOR M--
NO.
NO HARM IN ASKING.

YOU SAID SOMETHING ABOUT STEP *THREE?*
STEP THREE IS WE GET-

HELLGATE! COME.
IF IT'S ALL THE SAME TO YOU...I THINK I'D RATHER STAY RIGHT HERE.
YOU'RE COMING, ONE WAY OR--

ER...NO. THIS IS VERY BAD.
IS THIS STEP FOUR?
IF OUR DEMON JAILERS ARE LIKE HUMAN POLICE...
...THESE TWO ARE SPECIAL OPS.
THEY DON'T HAVE NAMES.
WE JUST CALL THEM ROCK AND BONE.

AND HOPED WE'D NEVER HAVE TO GO TOE-TO-TOE WITH THEM...
...LIKE WE'RE ABOUT TO.

WAIT.

I NEED THIS.
I DON'T GIVE A CRAP HOW SPECIAL THEY ARE...
...I NEED THE PRACTICE.

VROOM
VROOM
EXCELLENT!
C'MON, RIDER!
THUNK!
WE'RE GOING TO KILL YOU ALL AND WEAR YOUR ORGANS FOR TROPHIES AND TURN YOUR SKIN INTO BOOTS!
BUT THE RIDER...
...HE'S SPECIAL.
WE'RE GOING TO SUCK THE HELLFIRE OUT OF YOUR BONES...
...AND SPLIT YOUR SKULL DOWN THE MIDDLE, SO WE CAN SHARE.

KRAK
I THINK WE BROKE HIS JAW.
I AM GOING TO ADMIT TO BEING DISAPPOINTED.
I NEVER MET AN ACTUAL RIDER-- OTHER THAN OUR CURRENT BIG BOSS...
...BUT THEIR REP SEEMS A BIT UNDESERVED. I ALMOST DON'T WANT THE SKULL... ALMOST.
ARRRGH!
WHAT THE--?

THAT WASN'T AS MUCH FUN TO WATCH AS YOU MIGHT THINK. AND THE TALKATIVE ONE WAS STARTING TO BORE ME.
SO I HAMSTRUNG THEM.

THANKS. I HAD IT UNDER CONTROL.
I WAS JUST WAITING FOR THEM TO GET CLOSE ENOUGH SO I COULD DO...

...THIS!
FWOOSH

CLICK
STEP FOUR...?

STEP FOUR IS WE RIDE OUT OF HELL? AS SIMPLE AS THAT?
I NEVER SAID "SIMPLE," BUT THE SPOT WE NEED IS JUST AHEAD. WE'D GET THERE FASTER IF--
I ALREADY TOLD YOU THAT YOU'RE NOT RIDING ON MY BIKE. BUT I'M HAPPY TO DRAG YOU AS WELL.
ANYWAY... IT'S A WEAK SPOT BETWEEN THE DIMENSIONS. SOME SAY IT'S THE PLACE WHERE HELL WAS CREATED.
HOW DO YOU KNOW THIS STUFF?
YOU DO KNOW LILITH IS THE MOTHER, GRANDMOTHER, OR GREAT-GRANDMOTHE OF MOST OF THE DEMONS DOWN HERE, RIGHT?

SHE LIKED TO TALK. I LISTENED.
THERE'S A RITUAL... IT'S ACTUALLY HOW SHE ESCAPED FROM HELL A WHILE BACK. SHE USED AN ANCIENT LEVIATHAN.*
WE'LL HAVE TO IMPROVISE.
*SPIRITS OF VENGEANCE (1992) --MARK OF VENGEA

WHAT ABOUT ME?
DON'T WORRY, ANTON... WE COULDN'T POSSIBLY DO THIS WITHOUT YOU.
WHAT DOES THAT MEAN?
IT MEANS--

UGH!
SHUNK
END OF THE LINE, RIDER!

FRIEND OF YOURS?
I HAVE NO FRIENDS.
I'M SHOCKED.
IT'S GOING TO TAKE MORE THAN THIS TO KEEP ME HERE. I HAVE A MISSION...THINGS I'VE GOT TO DO... BACK ON--

HA!
MISSION?
YOU'RE NO RIDER ANY-MORE. YOU HAVE NO MISSION...NO MEANING...YOU JUST MOVE FORWARD ON PURE INSTINCT.

YOU'RE JUST ANOTHER USED-UP PIECE OF CRAP CAST INTO THE PITS OF HELL FOR US TO PLAY WITH.
AND WE CAME PREPARED TO PLAY!
WE CAN OUTRUN THEM. WE JUST HAVE TO GET TO THE END OF--
I DON'T WANT TO RUN. I WANT... VENGEANCE.
SERIOUSLY? YOU BARELY GOT THROUGH THE LAST TWO ALIVE. AT LEAST LEAVE HELLGATE WITH ME--
NO!!!
VROOOOM
WE NEED HIM IN ONE PIECE!
YOU HEARD HIM... RIGHT?
YOU NEED--

--MEEEEEE!
YOU'LL BE FINE, BUT...
VRDDDDDOM
...YOU'RE GOING TO WANT TO TENSE UP.
OH...I AM TENSE--
WAIT! WHAT?
ARE YOU @#%&#$ KIDDING ME?
LET ME KNOW, BUT DO NOT GET ANY ON MY LEATHERS.
RIGHT NOW, ALL THIS DEMON AND HELL CRAP IS PISSING ME OFF.
I KNOW YOU ALL THINK YOU KNOW US.
BLAZE, KETCH, ZARATHOS... WHOEVER.
WIMPS.
TCHUNK
THANKS FOR THE ASSIST, HELLGATE.
SEE YOU IN--WELL-- HERE!

I DON'T HAVE A SENSE OF HUMOR.
NO KIDDING... I THINK I'M GOING TO VOMIT.
CAN YOU VOMIT IN HELL?
LOOK AT THAT...I GUESS I *DO* HAVE A SENSE OF HUMOR.
NO! NOT THERE!
THOSE ARE *LITERALLY* THE BURNING PITS OF HELL! THEY'LL EVEN STRIP THE FLESH OFF OF--
GOOD THING I'M ALL *BONE!*
SPLASH
GLUB
GLUB
GLUB

CRAP! BADILINO'S CRAZY!
AND NOW HE'S DEAD!
WE'RE IN HELL, GENIUS!
WE'RE ALL CRAZY AND DEAD!
YOU ARE SUPPOSED TO BE A GENIUS, RIGHT? JUST WAIT.
GLUB
BLURB
BURBLE
VROOOM
HOW MUCH FARTHER?
OH... WE ARE HERE!
TIME FOR HELLGATE TO PROVE HIS WORTH...AND BE THE IMPROVISATION.
WAIT? WHAT?

CHIK
NO...NO... WAIT--
THOK THOK
ARRRGH!
THOK
THOK
WHY?
PRETTY SURE YOU WEREN'T GOING TO VOLUNTEER FOR THIS.
IS THE REST OF IT GOING TO BE AS PAINFUL?
VERY.

WHAT? YOU'RE NOT GOING TO... NO...YOU DON'T ACTUALLY THINK BECAUSE MY NAME IS **HELLGATE**...

LILITH HAD AN ANCIENT AND MASSIVE SEA CREATURE...WE'RE GOING TO MAKE DO WITH YOU.

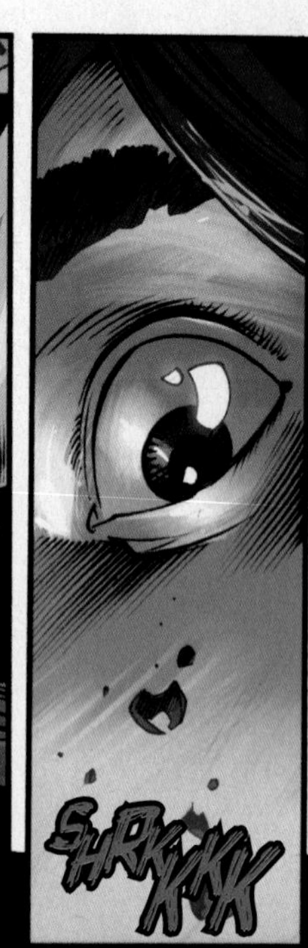
SHRKKKKK

NOOOOOOOOOO!
THAT'S A START. I JUST NEED TO OPEN IT UP A LOT MORE AND--
NO.
I'VE GOT THIS.

HELLGATE, I WANT YOU TO KNOW THAT THIS IS NOT JUST PAYBACK FOR WHAT YOU DID TO ME. **THIS** IS...

...VENGEANCE!

R-I-I-I-P!

CRAK!
RMMMBLE
KRAK
THOOM
THOOM
KTHOOM
BUT NOT FOR LONG.
I CAN FINISH THE BABYLONIAN AND ASSYRIAN CHANTS AS WE GO, BUT WE'VE GOT TO GO THROUGH TOGETHER.
I KNOW YOU DON'T WANT ANYONE ELSE ON YOUR BIKE, BUT--
GET ON.

EVERYTHING AFTER THIS IS A CRAPSHOOT.
FROM WHAT I UNDERSTAND, WE'RE GOING TO GO THROUGH SOME SERIOUS STUFF.
I'M GOING TO HAVE TO REALLY FOCUS TO GET US THROUGH. YOU DRIVE...I'LL STEER.

ALL AT ONCE, I CAN SEE EVERYTHING.
MY LIFE...SKINNER'S LIFE...ALL BLENDED TOGETHER.
MEPHISTO...GHOST RIDER...BLAZE...
EACH, IN THEIR OWN WAY, PUT ME ON MY PATH TO HELL.
SKINNER...
HE HAD A FAMILY... A HUMAN FAMILY...
A WIFE...A CHILD...
THEN THE DEMON QUEEN LILITH CALLED AND...
HOW COULD HE DO THAT?
HOW?

EW YORK CITY...
FZZZZZAT

THANKS FOR THE RIDE.
THAT WAS WEIRD, RIGHT?

SOMETHING WRONG?

I SAW WHAT YOU DID.
AH... MY WIFE AND LITTLE BOY.

I DID WHAT I HAD TO DO!
I LOVED THEM! THEY WERE MY HUMANITY. MOTHER WOULD HAVE TORTURED MY WIFE FOR AN ETERNITY BEFORE KILLING HER.
WORSE...MY SON...HE WAS OF MY BLOOD...SHE WOULD HAVE CAUSED THE DEMON IN HIM TO EMERGE AND MADE HIM ONE OF HER OWN.
WHAT I DID WAS AN ACT OF KINDNESS!

SO...
SPLUNCH

...IS THIS!
YOU CARRIED A SMALL SPLINTER OF HELLFIRE AROUND FOR YEARS.
LET'S SEE HOW MUCH YOU CAN HANDLE BEFORE...

NOOOO!

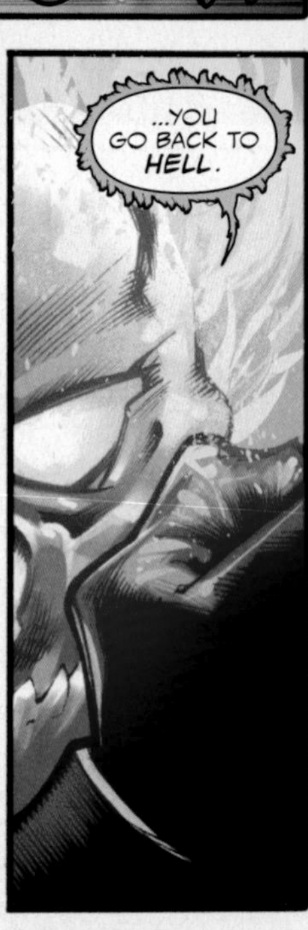

...YOU GO BACK TO HELL.

THIS IS A SECOND CHANCE FOR ME.
OR IS IT A THIRD?
NEVER GOING TO BE TOTALLY FREE FROM THE FORCES OF HELL THAT TURNED ME INTO THIS.
SO, I'VE GOT TO TWIST WHAT I'VE GOT TOWARD MY OWN AGENDA.
SCREW WHATEVER KETCH AND BLAZE ARE PLAYING AT.

WAS NEVER THEM... AND WANT NOTHING TO DO WITH HELL.
I'M STILL BADILINO... TILL DRAGGING AROUND LL THE SAME BAGGAGE OF MY LIFE.
LIFE SUCKS...IT'S MESSY...FILLED WITH PAIN AND SORROW...
PEOPLE ARE HURT, TORTURED, AND DIE AT THE HANDS OF OTHERS EVERY DAY.
THAT'S WHEN I COME IN.
THAT'S WHEN VENGEANCE RIDES!
END...?

GREETINGS, GHOST RIDER FANS, AND HOPE YOU ENJOYED--AT LAST--THE RETURN OF MICHAEL BADILINO!

This special issue began development over four years ago (!) and went through many iterations before blazing to life as the story you now hold in your hands. It's been a labor of love for Howard and Javier, as these giants of Ghost Rider lore plotted their return to the world of the Spirits of Vengeance, and for myself and the fantastic Marc, Arif, and Joe as we figured out and executed the return of Vengeance!

Many a discussion were had, debating where and how this special should take place--across different eras of Ghost Rider, featuring different players from the mythos, darting around changes between subsequent Ghost Rider series...but ultimately, the best time to set this was now--and with a character who'd been recently missing from Ghost Rider tales. And thus, Vengeance is back (with a, well, vengeance) in the present day of the Marvel Universe!

Once the plan was carved in stone and the appropriate souls sacrificed, Mr. Saltares set to work redefining Vengeance's look. Before we close out this volume, I'll turn it over to Howard, and to Javier, with a peek behind the curtain at Javier's sketches and designs!

See you in hell!
Mark Basso
November 2020

I'm sincerely hoping you enjoyed this issue of VENGEANCE as much as I enjoyed doing it.

It was a thrill to be called and asked to do it. First off, it was a great and nostalgic feeling to work with Howard Mackie again. As well as it was to work with Mark Basso for the first time.

(A truly patient editor, I can assure you. It takes a balanced soul to be able to negotiate their vision with others' creative input.)

Again, thank you for picking up the book and paying so I can play for a living.

Sincerely,
Javier Saltares

"You can take the boy out of the cemetery, but you can't take the cemetery out of the boy." Technically speaking, the first part of this classic statement (which I just made up) is only true if you are an 18th-century grave robber. I will tell you that I am the living (mostly) embodiment of the conclusion of the saying. I was born and raised in and around the cemeteries of Cypress Hills, Brooklyn. It's from those cemeteries I drew inspiration for the stories I created to add to the Ghost Rider mythos. So, I was thrilled when I was approached by Marvel to jump feetfirst back into hell and catch up with my old friends Javier Saltares and Michael Badilino.

I always had a soft spot--some would say "dark" spot--in my heart for Badilino and VENGEANCE. He--along with CARETAKER--are two characters I always wanted to explore just a little more. I always thought of Vengeance as what Ghost Rider would be like if he was not constrained by the kinder heart of his human host. You know… what if Ghost Rider wasn't such a wimp?

Having the opportunity to team back up with artist-extraordinaire Javier Saltares, and dipping my feet back into some puddles of hellfire, was something I couldn't pass up. A very special thanks to editor Mark Basso for helping me find my way back to hell, nudging me when I needed nudging, and for listening to all my stories of "back in the OLD DAYS when we used to have to cut down the trees and use our own blood to make the ink for the comic books we produced." He really is one of the best!

Hope you enjoy the ride we took together. Now--I've got to clean some dirt out from under my fingernails. I PROMISE it probably didn't come from a graveyard--Caretaker would never allow THAT.

Howard "Not Dead Yet" Mackie
November 2020

SPIRITS OF GHOST RIDER: MOTHER OF DEMONS
VARIANT BY **STEPHANIE HANS**

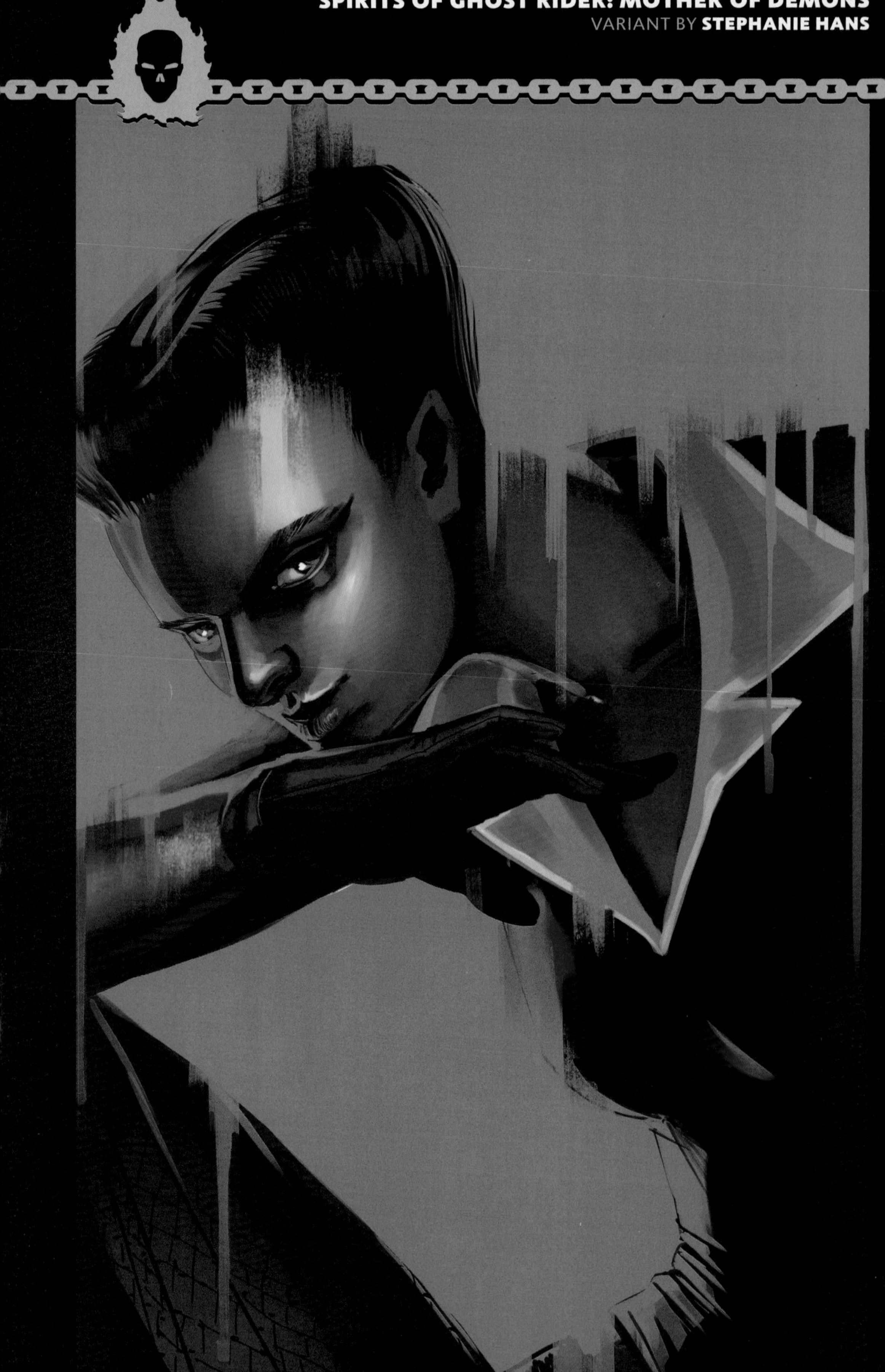

DESIGN VARIANT BY **AARON KUDER**

GHOST RIDER: KING IN BLACK
WOMEN'S HISTORY MONTH VARIANT BY JEN BARTEL
MARVEL
$4.99
WOMEN'S HISTORY
KUSHALA
EST. 2016
#1
VARIANT EDITION
JEN BARTEL

VARIANT BY **GERALD PAREL**

GHOST RIDER: RETURN OF VENGEANCE
VARIANT BY RYAN STEGMAN & FRANK MARTIN

GHOST RIDER: RETURN OF VENGEANCE
HIDDEN GEM VARIANT BY RON GARNEY, CHRIS IVY & PAUL MOUNTS
RON GARNEY/C. IVY

KNULLIFIED VARIANT BY **KYLE HOTZ** & **DAN BROWN**

GHOST RIDER: RETURN OF VENGEANCE

PAGES 6-7 PENCILS & INKS BY **JAVIER SALTARES**

GHOST RIDER: RETURN OF VENGEANCE
PAGES 8-9 PENCILS & INKS BY JAVIER SALTARES

GHOST RIDER: RETURN OF VENGEANCE

PAGES 10-11 PENCILS BY **JAVIER SALTARES**
& INKS BY **JAVIER SALTARES** & **MARC DEERING**

GHOST RIDER: RETURN OF VENGEANCE

PAGES 12-13 PENCILS BY **JAVIER SALTARES** & INKS BY **MARC DEERING**

AGES 14-15 PENCILS BY **JAVIER SALTARES** & INKS BY **MARC DEERING**

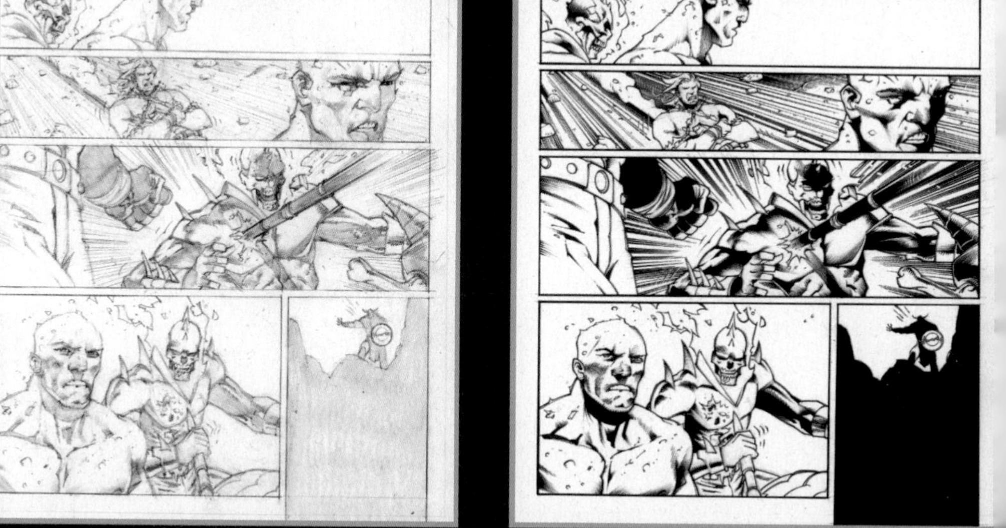

GHOST RIDER: RETURN OF VENGEANCE

PAGES 16-17 PENCILS BY **JAVIER SALTARES** & INKS BY **MARC DEERING**

GHOST RIDER: RETURN OF VENGEANCE

PAGES 18-19 PENCILS BY **JAVIER SALTARES** & INKS BY **MARC DEERING**

GHOST RIDER: RETURN OF VENGEANCE

PAGES 20-21 PENCILS BY **JAVIER SALTARES** & INKS BY **MARC DEERING**

AGES 22-23 PENCILS BY JAVIER SALTARES & INKS BY MARC DEERING

PAGE 24 PENCILS BY **JAVIER SALTARES** & INKS BY **MARC DEERI**

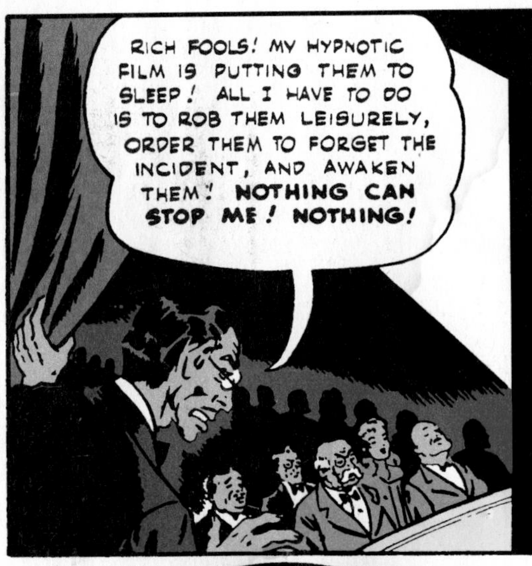
RICH FOOLS! MY HYPNOTIC FILM IS PUTTING THEM TO SLEEP! ALL I HAVE TO DO IS TO ROB THEM LEISURELY, ORDER THEM TO FORGET THE INCIDENT, AND AWAKEN THEM! **NOTHING CAN STOP ME! NOTHING!**

SO NOW WE KNOW THE WILY WRITER'S SHREWD STRATEGY! BUT AT THAT MOMENT...
WHAT--? **BATMAN** AND **ROBIN!**

NOW SHOWING!
IN PERSON!
EXIT

OVER THE HEADS OF THE STARTLED AUDIENCE SWOOPS THE DYNAMIC DUO!
A CLEVER PLOT, BUT YOUR ENDING ISN'T GOOD ENOUGH. WE'LL HAVE TO GIVE YOU A REJECTION... AND THIS TIME YOU'RE NOT SLIPPING FREE!

A SWIFT SUMMONS BRINGS THE POLICE RUSHING TO THE SCENE...
BUT HOW DID YOU KNOW MY SCHEME? WHAT MADE YOU BRING ANOTHER FILM TO REPLACE MY HYPNOTIC MOVIE?
THAT'S EASY! AUTHORS OFTEN USE PET PHRASES... AND YOU USED "THE MOST TIRESOME MOVIE EVER MADE" IN ONE OF YOUR EARLIER NOVELS! IT WAS THE SAME PLAN AS THE ONE YOU USED TONIGHT!
LATER, AT HOME...
SO BRAMWELL PLAGIARIZED FROM ONE OF HIS OWN BOOKS! WELL, THAT'S A PRETTY GOOD ENDING FOR THE **CRIME OF THE MONTH!**
YES... BUT BRAMWELL IS JUST BEGINNING A NEW CHAPTER!

BAH! THEY WON'T KEEP ME HERE LONG!
ONLY ABOUT TWENTY YEARS!
PRISONER OF THE MONTH
STOP KICKING, BRAMWELL! A FAMOUS WRITER LIKE YOU OUGHT TO BE USED TO PENS!
THE END

HE CAN'T GET AWAY FROM THE BATPLANE AND THE BATMOBILE BOTH!
ABOARD THE BATPLANE, THE MANTLED MANHUNTER FLASHES SKYWARD... AND A FEW MINUTES LATER...
THERE'S ROBIN! BUT NOT A TRACE OF BRAMWELL! HE MUST'VE TAKEN A PRIVATE ROAD THROUGH THE WOODS TO BE SHIELDED FROM THE TREES!
EYES NARROWED, THE HOODED SLEUTH PONDERS A SINGLE SLIM CLUE...
SO BRAMWELL'S CRIME OF THE MONTH WILL BE THE SOCIAL EVENT OF THE YEAR, EH? HMM... THAT FITS THE ALLIED WAR RELIEF DRIVE THAT SOCIETY IS GIVING TONIGHT! AND THAT PHRASE, "THE MOST TIRESOME MOVIE EVER MADE," IS FAMILIAR! WHERE DID I COME ACROSS IT BEFORE---?
MEANWHILE, IN A TREE-SHADOWED LANE FAR FROM MYSTERY CASTLE...
THOSE SIMPLETONS WILL NEVER FIND ME! AND NOW TO WIN THE BIGGEST PRIZE... THE LOOT THOSE IGNORANT GANGSTERS GARNERED--ALL FOR ME!
AND THAT NIGHT, AT SOCIETY'S GLITTERING WAR RELIEF DRIVE...
LADIES AND GENTLEMEN, MR. BRAMWELL B. BRAMWELL, THE FAMOUS MYSTERY WRITER, WILL NOW HONOR US WITH A PRIVATE SHOWING OF AN EXPERIMENTAL MOVIE HE HAS MADE! LIGHTS OUT, PLEASE!
YOU ARE SLEEPY... YOU ARE FALLING A-S-L-E-E-P...
GOODNESS I'M GETTING SO DROWSY!
I CAN HARDLY KEEP MY EYES OPEN!
12